FEB 09

THE POLICE STATION

David and Patricia Armentrout

Rourke

Publishing LLC
Vero Beach, Florida 32964

www.rourkepublishing.com

PHOTO CREDITS: © Jim Parkin: page 4, 20; © Cary Kalscheuer: page 5; © Jack Dagley Photography: page 6; © G. Goodman: page 7; © Gary Blakeley; © Jacom Stephens: page 8; © Karen Lau: page 9; © Jeff Thrower: page 10; © A. William Caleno: page 11; © Kanwarjit Singh Boparai: page 12; © Harry Hu: page 13; © Dragan Trifunovic: page 14; © Pruitt: page 15; © Mike Clarke: page 16; © Rorem: page 17; © Graham Taylor: page 18; © Christine Glade: page 19; © Kevin R. Williams: page 21; © David P. Lewis: page 22;

Edited by Kelli Hicks

Cover design by Teri Intzegian
Interior design by Teri Intzegian

Library of Congress Cataloging-in-Publication Data

Armentrout, David, 1962-
   The police department / David and Patricia Armentrout.
      p. cm. -- (Our community)
   ISBN 978-1-60472-339-7
   1. Police--Juvenile literature. I. Armentrout, Patricia, 1960- II. Title.
   HV7922.A75 2009
   363.2--dc22
                              2008016349

Printed in the USA

CG/CG

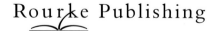

Rourke Publishing

www.rourkepublishing.com – rourke@rourkepublishing.com
Post Office Box 3328, Vero Beach, FL 32964

Table of Contents

Community Police

Your community includes neighbors, classmates, and others who live, work, and play nearby. Police officers are members of the community, too.

Police officers keep
order and enforce **laws**.

Police work can be demanding and dangerous. Officers must be **healthy, strong, and brave.**

A police officer makes an arrest.

There are more
than 800,000
police officers
in the
United States.

Police officers learn
through training.

Community police wear uniforms. They dress alike so **everyone knows who they are.**

People feel safe
when police patrol
community events.

Emergencies

Police officers are trained emergency **responders**. They are often the first to arrive at the scene of an accident.

Police look for the cause of a truck accident.

Police direct traffic away from a search and rescue team.

On Patrol

Most police officers **patrol** in cars or on motorcycles. Police vehicles are well marked and easily seen.

Police cars have flashing lights and loud sirens.

Motorcycle police lead a community parade.

In big cities, police patrol on foot, on bikes, and even on horseback. Getting around this way brings them closer to the people in their community.

Police patrol high-crime areas on bicycles.

Trained police horses move safely through city traffic.

Special Vehicles

Sometimes police use special vehicles. Large police departments have boats, planes, and helicopters.

Boats patrol local waterways.

Wherever criminals go, police can go, too.

Officers follow the action
in a police helicopter.

Behind the Scenes

Some police officers work at the station. They monitor traffic, take calls, and use computers to track down information.

A big police department
is a busy place.

Best Friends

People say dogs are man's best friends. A dog can also be an officer's best friend. Dogs help police do their job.

Police dogs use their sense of smell to find missing people.

Trained police dogs show off
for the community.

Law and Order

Laws are rules that people live by. Police officers enforce community laws.

Police officers make sure communities are safe places to live.

Glossary

criminals (KRIM-uh-nuhlz): people who break laws

laws (LAWZ): rules that govern a community

patrol (puj-TROHL): to travel around an area keeping watch on people

responders (ri-SPOND-erz): people who react quickly to something

INDEX

FURTHER READING

Apte, Sunita. *Police Horses.* Bearport Publishing, 2007.

Braithwaite, Jill. *Police Cars.* Lerner Publications, 2004.

Ruffin, Francis E. *Police Dogs.* Bearport Publishing, 2005.

WEBSITES

www.ou.edu/oupd/kidsafe/start.htm

www.mcgruff.org

ABOUT THE AUTHORS

David and Patricia Armentrout specialize in nonfiction children's books. They enjoy exploring different topics and have written about many subjects, including sports, animals, history, and people. David and Patricia love to spend their free time outdoors with their two boys and dog Max.